30 POWERFUL WORSHIP SONGS FROM TODAY'S TOP ARTISTS

"No part of this publication may be reproduced or transmitted in any form or by any means, electronic or mechanical, including photocopy, recording or any information storage and retrieval system, without permission in writing from the publisher."

   in association with

© MMIII Brentwood-Benson Music Publishing, Inc., 741 Cool Springs Blvd., Franklin, TN 37067. All rights reserved.
Unauthorized duplication prohibited. DISTRIBUTED BY PROVIDENT MUSIC DISTRIBUTION, INC.

CONTENTS

Awesome God

Words and Music by
RICH MULLINS

© Copyright 1988 BMG Songs, Inc. (ASCAP).
All rights reserved. Used by permission.

* 1st time play whole note C chord, then fade.

Breathe

Words and Music by
MARIE BARNETT

© Copyright 1995 Mercy/Vineyard Publishing (ASCAP).
All rights reserved. Used by permission.

God of Wonders

Words and Music by
STEVE HINDALONG and
MARC BYRD

Lord of heav-en and earth,

Lord of all cre-a-tion,

Lord of heav-en and earth.

© Copyright 2000 New Spring Publishing, Inc. / Never Say Never Songs (ASCAP) (Administered by Brentwood-Benson Music Publishing, Inc.) / Meaux Mercy / Storm Boy Music (BMI) (Administered by EMI Christian Music Publishing). All rights reserved. Used by permission.

2nd time to Coda

God of won - ders be - yond our gal - ax - y, You are

ho - ly,____ ho - ly.____

Pre - cious Lord,____ re - veal Your____ heart____ to____ me. Fa - ther,

Ho - ly, ho - ly, ho - ly!

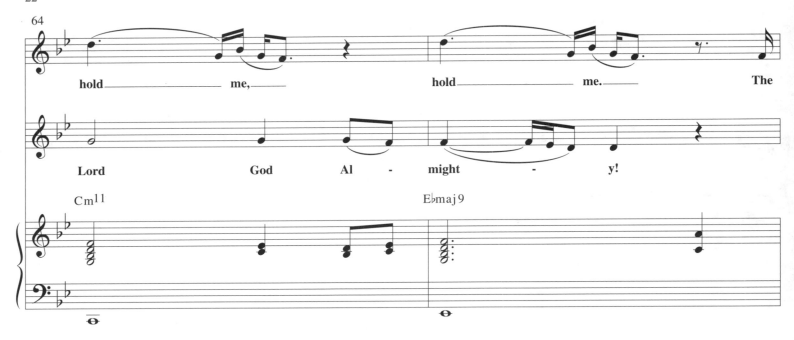

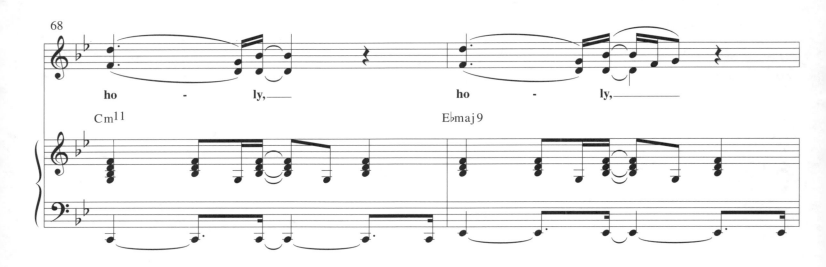

Imagine

**Words and Music by
AMY GRANT and
BART MILLARD**

© Copyright 2002 Grant Girls Music, LLC (ASCAP) (Administered by The Loving Company) / Simpleville Music (ASCAP) (Administered by Fun Attic Music).
All rights reserved. Used by permission.

face   is look - in' at_____ me._____   Sur -

round - ed by__ Your glo - ry,   what will   my__ heart feel?__   Will I__

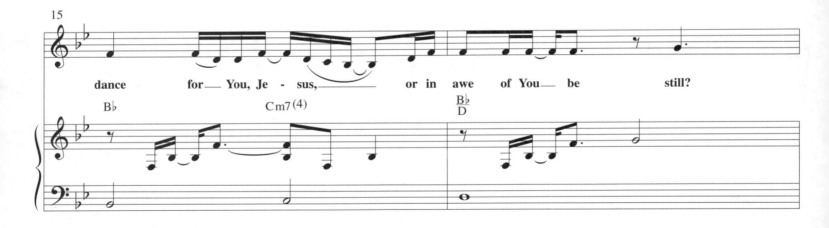

dance   for__ You, Je - sus,_____ or in awe of You__ be   still?

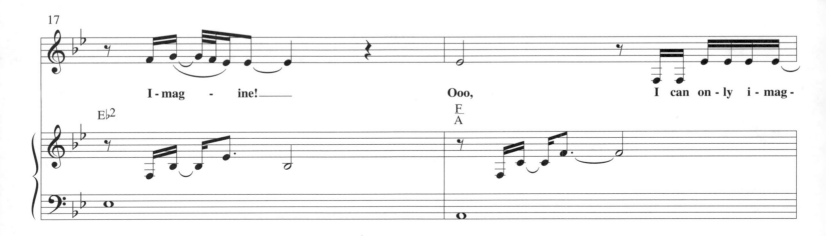

I - mag - ine!_____   Ooo,   I can on - ly i - mag -

44

Gm7   F   B♭(♯4) B♭(no3)   C

47   *f*

Fsus   F   C/E   Gm7   Fsus   F

Sur -

49

round - ed by___ for - give - ness, what will___ my___ heart feel?___ Will I dance___

B♭2   F/B♭   C

f

51

___ for You, Je - sus,   or in awe of You___ be still?___ Will I___

F   F2   F   F2   F

Majesty

**Words and Music by
JACK HAYFORD**

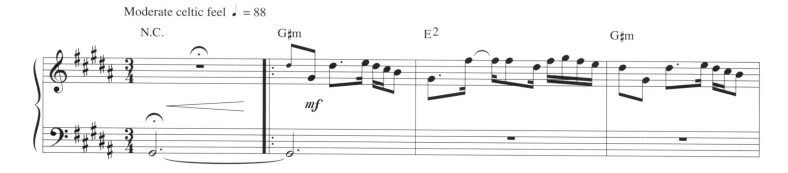

© Copyright 1980 Rocksmith Music (ASCAP) (Administered by Brentwood-Benson Music Publishing, Inc.).
All rights reserved. Used by permission.

34

You Are My All in All

Words and Music by
DENNIS JERNIGAN

© Copyright 1991 Shepherd's Heart Music, Inc. (BMI).
All rights reserved. Used by permission.

40

I Could Sing of Your Love Forever

Words and Music by
MARTIN SMITH

© Copyright 1994 Curious? Music UK (PRS) (Administered by EMI Christian Music Publishing).
All rights reserved. Used by permission.

Hungry (Falling on My Knees)

Words and Music by
KATHRYN SCOTT

Acoustic feel ♩ = 78

1. Hun - gry, I___ come to___ You, for___ I___ know
2. Bro - ken, I___ run to___ You, for___ Your___ arms___

___ You sat - is - fy.___ I am emp - ty,___ but
___ are o - pen wide.___ I am wea - ry,___ but

© Copyright 1999 Vineyard Songs (UK/EIRE) (Administered by Mercy/Vineyard Publishing in North America [ASCAP]).
All rights reserved. Used by permission.

(cues 2nd time)

Je - sus, You're all this heart is liv - ing for.

1.

2.
And I'm fall -

Hun - gry, I come to

You, for I know You sat - is - fy.

Forever

Words and Music by
CHRIS TOMLIN

© Copyright 2001 worshiptogether.com songs (ASCAP) / Six Steps Music (WTS) (Administered by EMI Christian Music Publishing).
All rights reserved. Used by permission.

You Are My King (Amazing Love)

Words and Music by
BILLY JAMES FOOTE

© Copyright 1999 worshiptogether.com songs (ASCAP) (Administered by EMI Christian Music Publishing).
All rights reserved. Used by permission.

I Give You My Heart

Words and Music by
REUBEN MORGAN

© Copyright 1995 Reuben Morgan / Hillsong Publishing (ASCAP) (Administered in the US and Canada by Integrity's Hosanna! Music)
(c/o Integrity Media, Inc., 1000 Cody Road, Mobile, AL 36695). All rights reserved. Used by permission.

Every Move I Make

Words and Music by
DAVID RUIS

© Copyright 1996 Mercy/Vineyard Publishing (ASCAP).
All rights reserved. Used by permission.

Let Everything That Has Breath

Words and Music by
MATT REDMAN

© Copyright 1999 Thankyou Music (PRS) (Administered by EMI Christian Music Publishing).
All rights reserved. Used by permission.

Redeemer

Words and Music by
NICOLE C. MULLEN

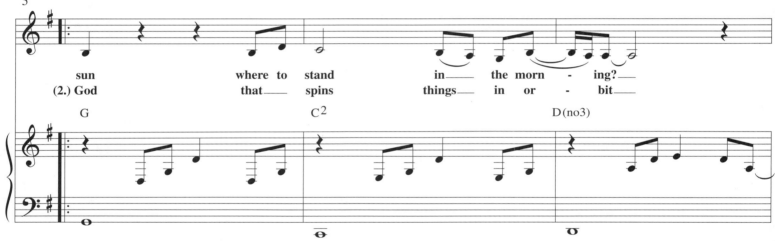

© Copyright 2000 Lil' Jas' Music (SESAC) (Administered by Wordspring Music, Inc.) / Wordspring Music, Inc. (SESAC).
All rights reserved. Used by permission.

Thy Word

Words and Music by
MICHAEL W. SMITH and
AMY GRANT

© Copyright 1984 Meadowgreen Music Company (ASCAP) (Administered by EMI Christian Music Publishing) / Word Music, Inc. (ASCAP).
All rights reserved. Used by permission.

Step by Step

**Words and Music by
BEAKER**

© Copyright 1991 BMG Songs, Inc. / Kid Brothers of St. Frank Publishing (ASCAP) (Administered by BMG Songs, Inc.).
All rights reserved. Used by permission.

Audience of One

Words and Music by
MICHAEL WEAVER

© Copyright 2000 Open Worship Music, Inc. (ASCAP) (Administered by ICG).
All rights reserved. Used by permission.

110

So what could I___ bring___
to hon - or Your___ maj -
- es - ty?
What song could I___ sing___
that would move the heart___ of___

Your Love, Oh Lord

Words and Music by
TAI ANDERSON, BRAD AVERY, DAVID CARR,
MARK D. LEE and MAC POWELL

© Copyright 1999 New Spring Publishing, Inc. / Vandura 2500 Songs (ASCAP) (Administered by Brentwood-Benson Music Publishing, Inc.).
All rights reserved. Used by permission.

123

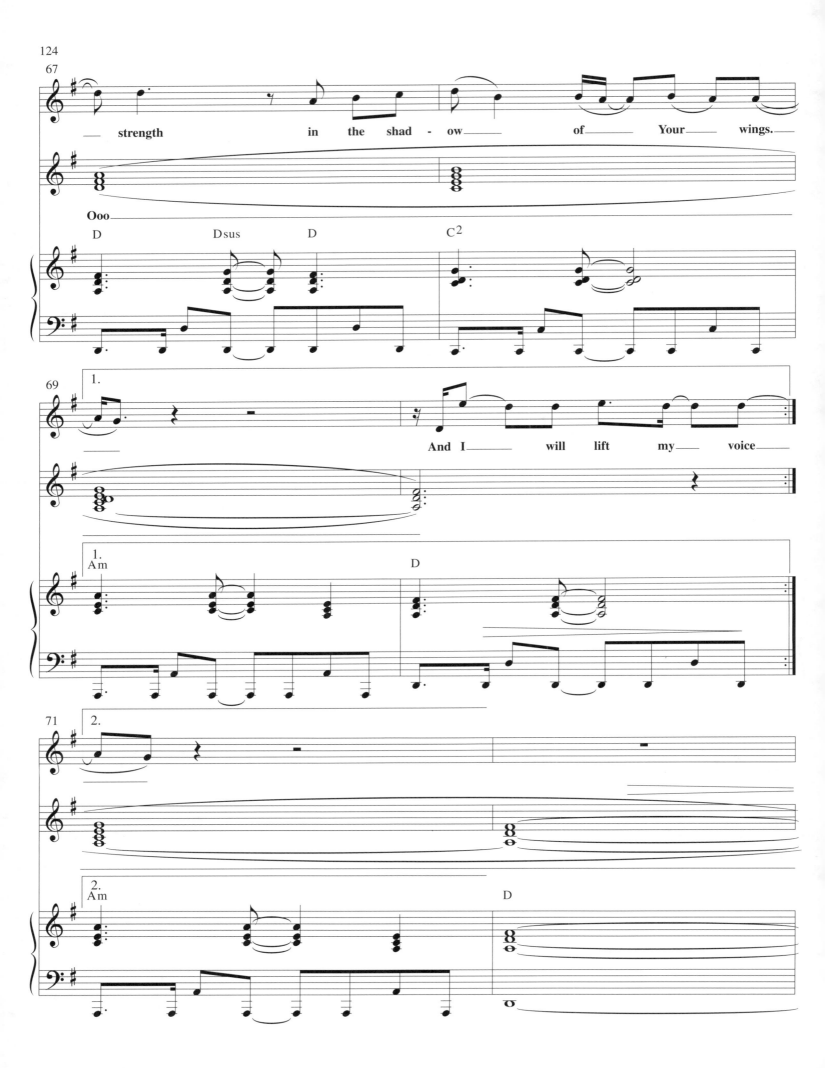

Your— love,— oh— Lord,——— reach - es to the heav -

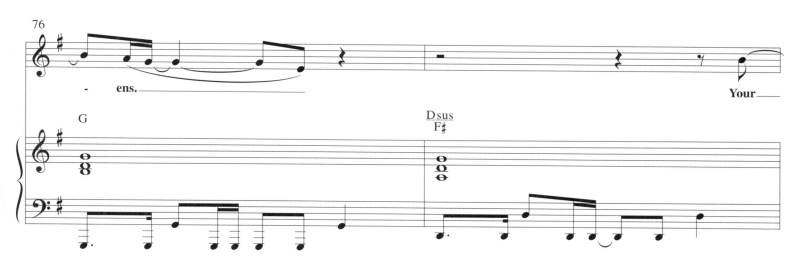

- ens.——— Your——

faith - ful - ness——— stretch - es to the skies.———

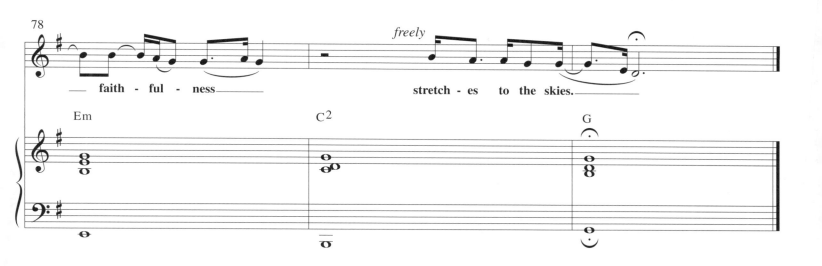

Shout to the Lord

Words and Music by
DARLENE ZSCHECH

© Copyright 1993 Darlene Zschech / Hillsong Publishing (ASCAP) (Administered in the US and Canada by Integrity's Hosanna! Music)
(c/o Integrity Media, Inc., 1000 Cody Road, Mobile, AL 36695). All rights reserved. Used by permission.

More Love, More Power

Words and Music by
JUDE DEL HIERRO

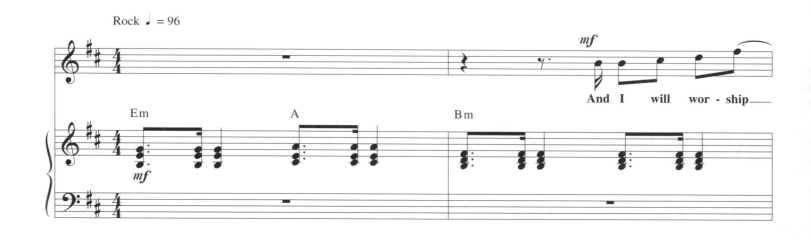

© Copyright 1987 Mercy/Vineyard Publishing (ASCAP).
All rights reserved. Used by permission.

132

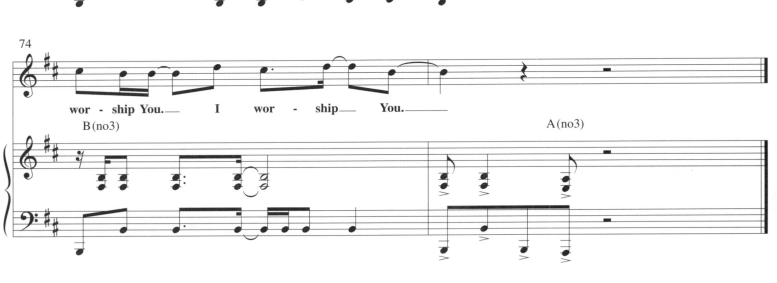

Here I Am to Worship

Words and Music by
TIM HUGHES

Worshipfully ♩ = 76

mp

Light of the World, You stepped down in-to dark - ness, o - pened my eyes, let me—

E   B   F♯m7   E   B

— see   beau - ty that made this— heart a - dore— You,

A2   E   B   F♯m7

hope of a life spent with— You.—   Here I am to

E   B   A2

© Copyright 2001 Thankyou Music (PRS) (Administered by EMI Christian Music Publishing).
All rights reserved. Used by permission.

140

142

In Christ Alone

Words and Music by
KEITH GETTY and
STUART TOWNEND

© Copyright 2002 Thankyou Music (PRS) (Administered by EMI Christian Music Publishing).
All rights reserved. Used by permission.

148

150

Draw Me Close

**Words and Music by
KELLY CARPENTER**

© Copyright 1994 Mercy/Vineyard Publishing (ASCAP).
All rights reserved. Used by permission.

152

nev - er let___ me go.___

I lay it all___ down___ a - gain,___ oh, oh,___

to hear You say___ that I'm Your friend.

You are my___ de - sire;___

The Happy Song

Words and Music by
MARTIN SMITH

© Copyright 1994 Curious? Music UK (PRS) (Administered by EMI Christian Music Publishing).
All rights reserved. Used by permission.

160

55
D/F♯
D
Em
57
Oh,
I could sing un -
C
G
59
end - ing songs of how You saved my
D/F♯
D
Em
61
soul.
Well, I could dance a
C
G

3rd time to Coda

thou - sand miles be - cause of___ Your great love.___

Oh, ev - 'ry - bod - y!

Better Is One Day

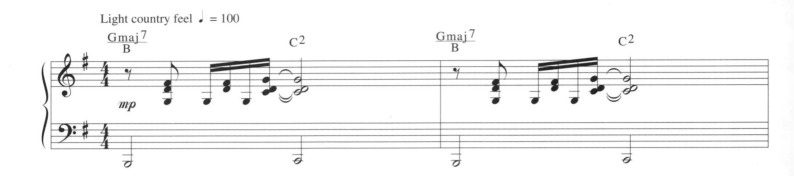

Words and Music by
MATT REDMAN

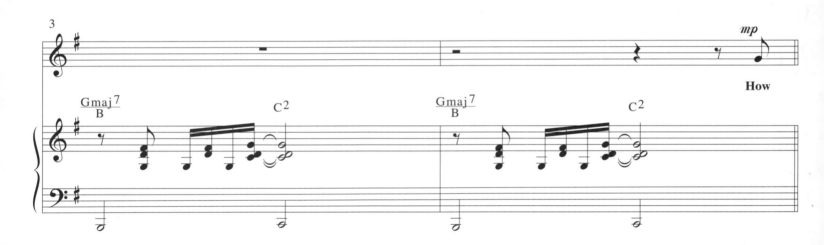

© Copyright 1995 Thankyou Music (PRS) (Administered by EMI Christian Music Publishing).
All rights reserved. Used by permission.

(2nd time: play bass notes in quarters)

1.

- where._____ One

F2 C2 D7

2.

- where._____

F2 C2 D7

My heart and flesh cry out___ to You, the Liv - ing God.___

Em D C D

Your Spir - it's wa - ter to my___ soul.___

Em D C D

Come, Now Is the Time to Worship

Words and Music by
BRIAN DOERKSEN

© Copyright 1998 Vineyard Songs (UK/EIRE) (Administered by Mercy/Vineyard Publishing in North America [ASCAP]).
All rights reserved. Used by permission.

180

The Heart of Worship

Words and Music by
MATT REDMAN

© Copyright 1999 Thankyou Music (PRS) (Administered by EMI Christian Music Publishing).
All rights reserved. Used by permission.

The Wonderful Cross

Words and Music by
**JESSE REEVES, CHRIS TOMLIN,
J.D. WALT and ISAAC WATTS**

© Copyright 2000 worshiptogether.com songs (ASCAP) / Six Steps Music (WTS) (Administered by EMI Christian Music Publishing).
All rights reserved. Used by permission.

He Is Exalted

Words and Music by
TWILA PARIS

© Copyright 1985 Straightway Music / Mountain Spring Music (ASCAP) (Administered by EMI Christian Music Publishing).
All rights reserved. Used by permission.

Be Thou My Vision

Traditional
Arranged by
DAN HASELTINE, CHARLIE LOWELL,
STEPHEN MASON and MATT ODMARK

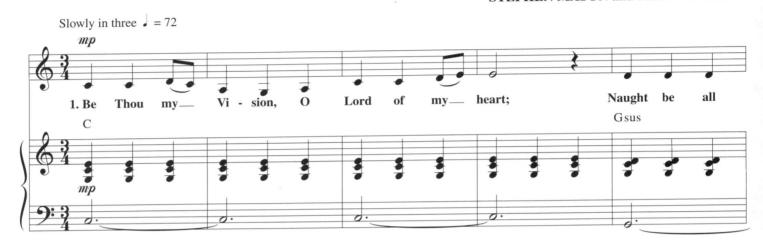

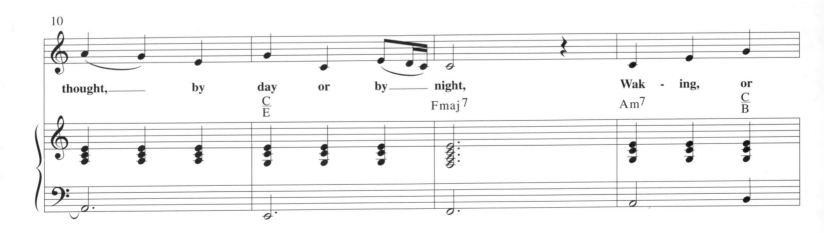

Arr. © Copyright 2003 Bridge Building Music, Inc. / Pogostick Music (BMI) (Administered by Brentwood-Benson Music Publishing, Inc.).
All rights reserved. Used by permission.

204

Oh Lord, You're Beautiful

Words and Music by
KEITH GREEN

© Copyright 1980 BMG Songs / Birdwing Music (ASCAP) (Administered by EMI Christian Music Publishing).
All rights reserved. Used by permission.

I Stand Amazed

Words and Music by
MARC BYRD and
CHRISTINE GLASS

© Copyright 2002 Meaux Mercy (BMI) (Administered by EMI Christian Music Publishing).
All rights reserved. Used by permission.

214

stand - ing at___ the cross___ where I'm sur - round - ed by___ Your grace,___ and I

mar - vel at___ the won - der of___ Your love.___ And I stand a -

___ Well, there is life in___ His bod - y. There is

Our Love Is Loud

**Words and Music by
DAVID CROWDER**

© Copyright 2002 worshiptogether.com songs (ASCAP) / Six Steps Music (WTS) (Administered by EMI Christian Music Publishing).
All rights reserved. Used by permission.